Acknowledgement of Country

We acknowledge the traditional custodians of the lands we work and on which this book was produced, and pay our respects to elders past, present and emerging. We recognise that sovereignty was never ceded. Always was and always will be. Aboriginal land.

For AJ, Jaiyana, Sienna, Savannah, and Ezekiel.

May you never forget who you are

and where you come from.

Copyright © 2022 by Gabriel Faatau'uu-Satiu. 809219

All rights reserved. No part of this book may be reproduced or transmitted in any form or by any means, electronic or mechanical, including photocopying, recording, or by any information storage and retrieval system, without permission in writing from the copyright owner.

This is a work of fiction. Names, characters, places and incidents either are the product of the author's imagination or are used fictitiously, and any resemblance to any actual persons, living or dead, events, or locales is entirely coincidental.

To order additional copies of this book, contact:
Xlibris
844-714-8691
www.Xlibris.com
Orders@Xlibris.com

ISBN: Softcover   978-1-6698-3183-9
       EBook   978-1-6698-3182-2

Print information available on the last page

Rev. date: 10/15/2022

WHERE I'M FROM

Gabriel Faatau'uu-Satiu

Illustrations by Daniel Majan

I'm from *koko* brown skin,

adorned with a *siapo*,

grounded like the soil from the *fanua*

and fragrant like the *popo* that nourishes me.

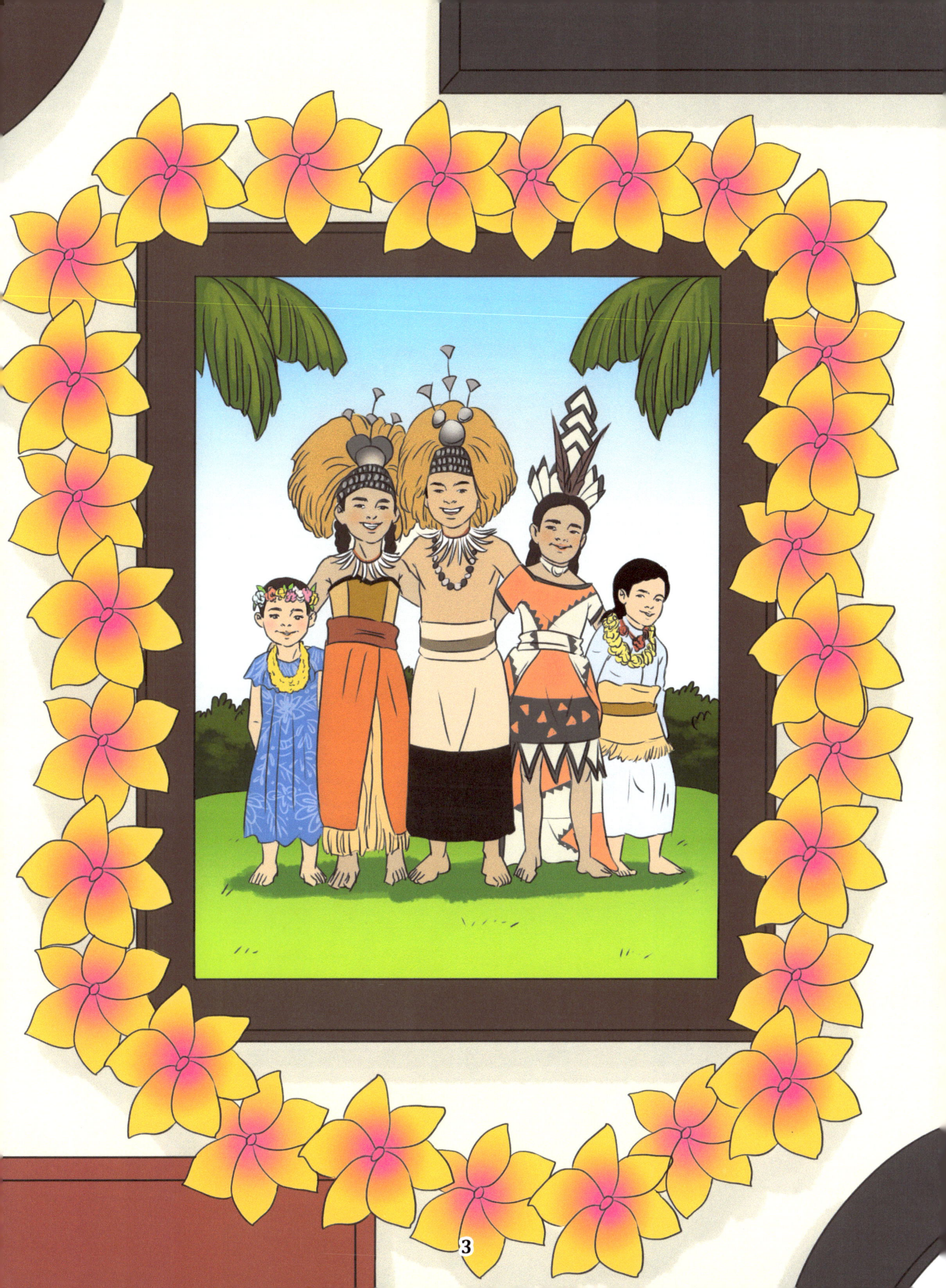

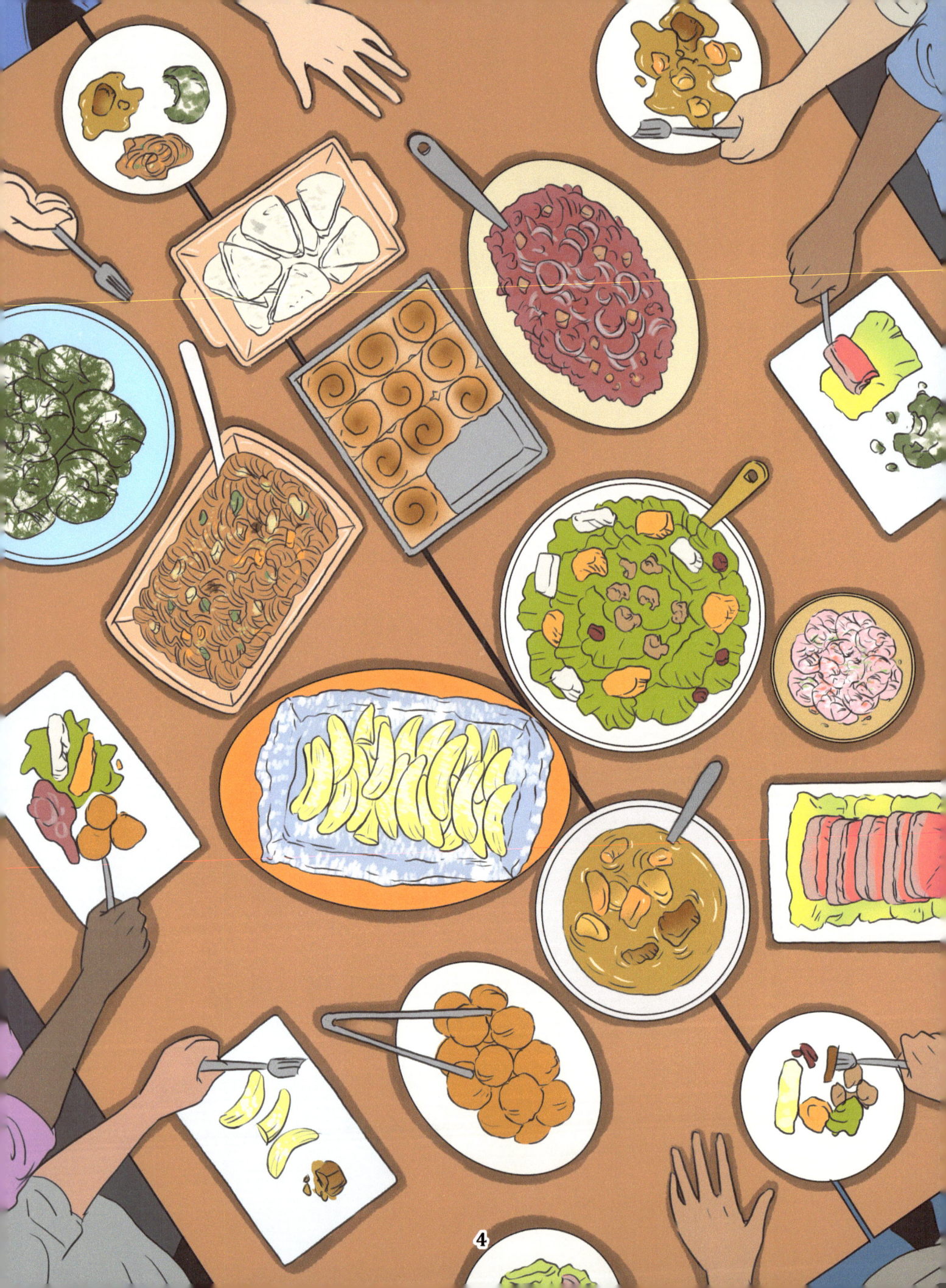

I'm from Sunday *to'ona'i* at Grandma's,
served from cans of *pisupo*, bowls of *oka*,
palusami accompanied with Dad's *fa'alifu fa'i*
and Mum's one-of-a-kind *sapasui*.

I'm from thick black hair,

with waves like the seas my ancestors voyaged,

shiny as the stars they navigated

and darker than the depths of *Te moana nui a Kiwa*.

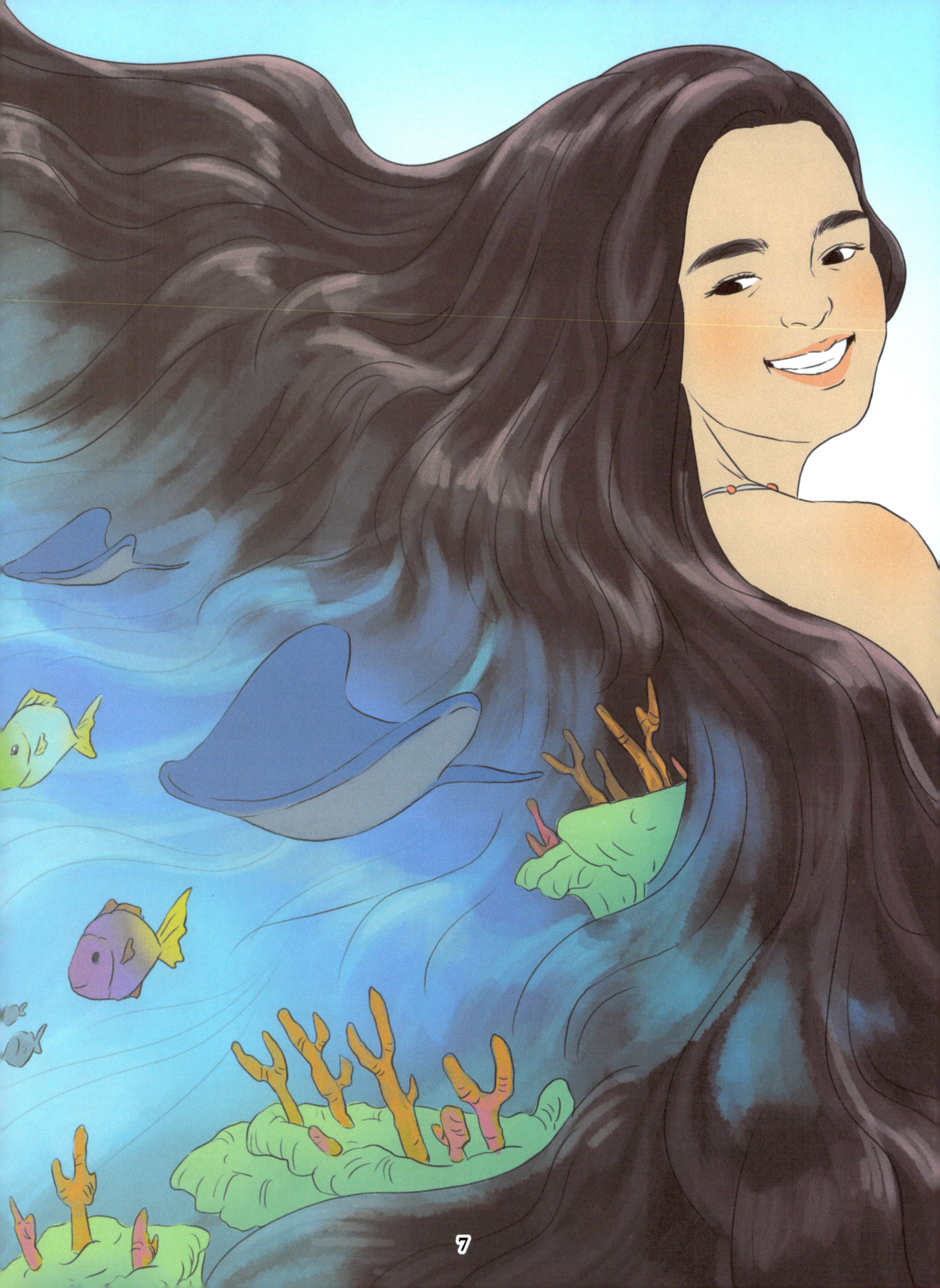

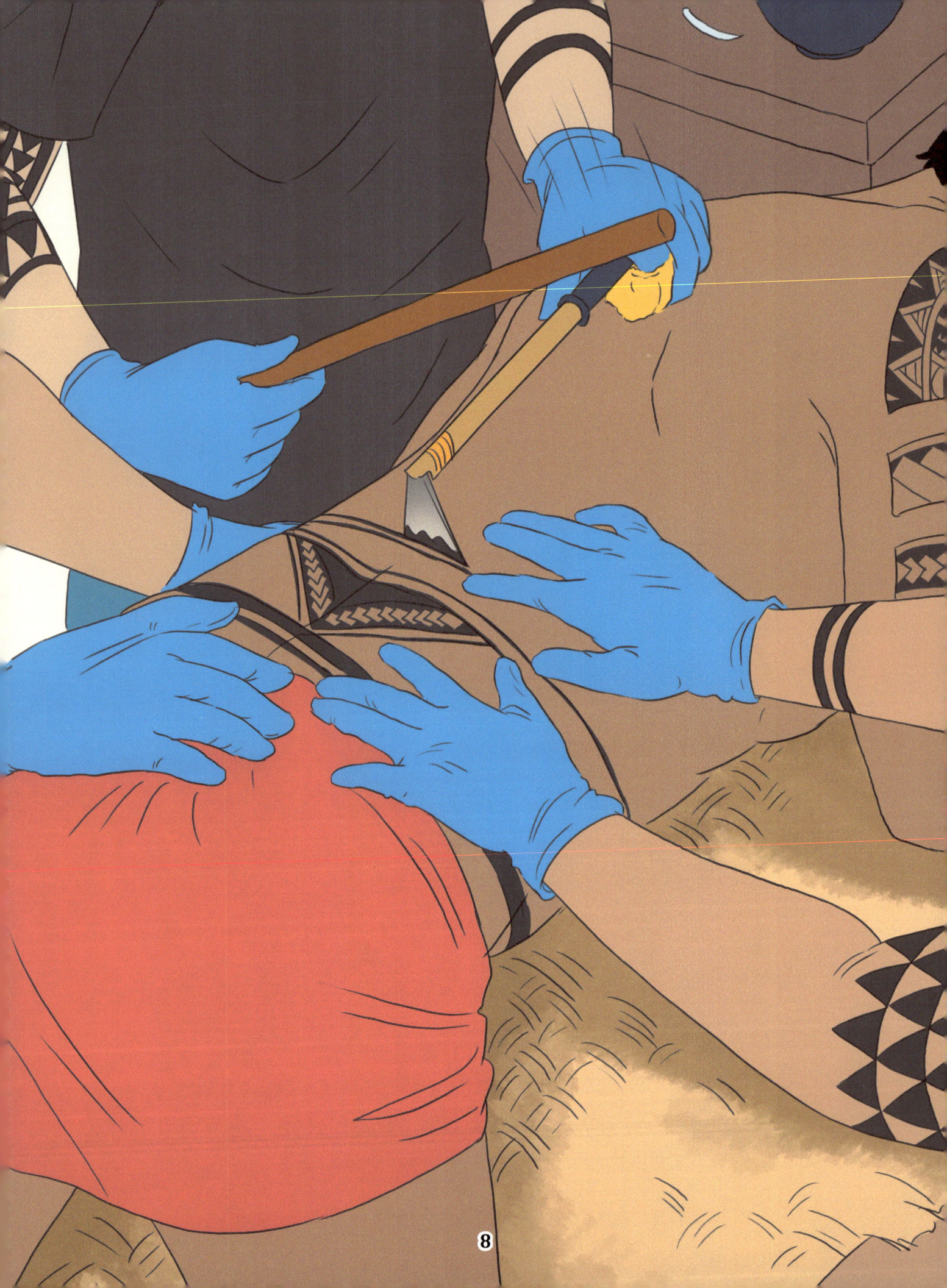

I'm from markings by the *tufuga*,

who are protectors of my heritage,

as they glisten with pride in my culture

each time the *sausau* strikes the *au*.

I'm from *pese* and *siva*,

gracefully *ifo* to say *fa'afetai lava*,

telling stories through my movement and words

while crowned with the *tuiga* from my foremothers and forefathers.

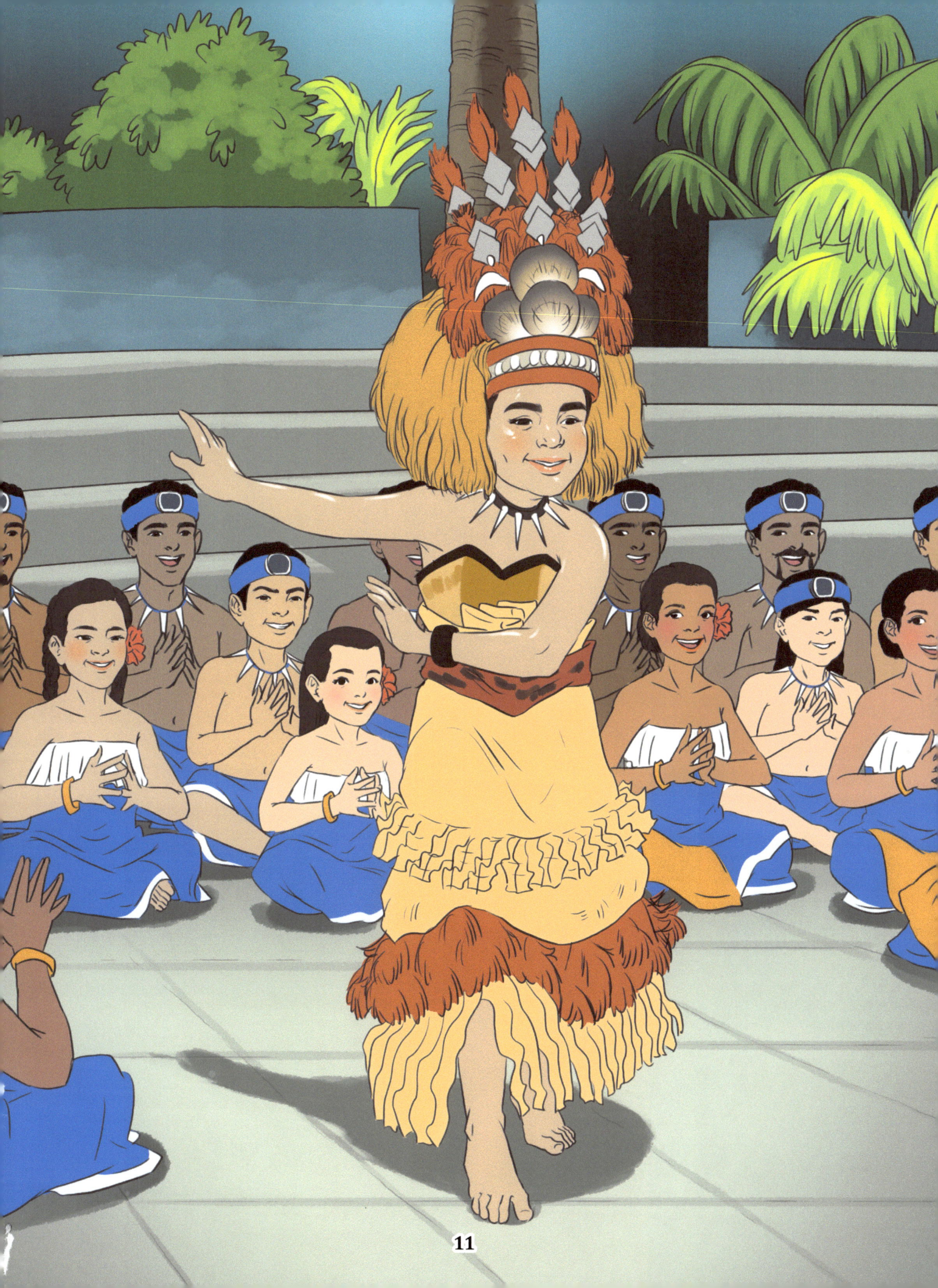

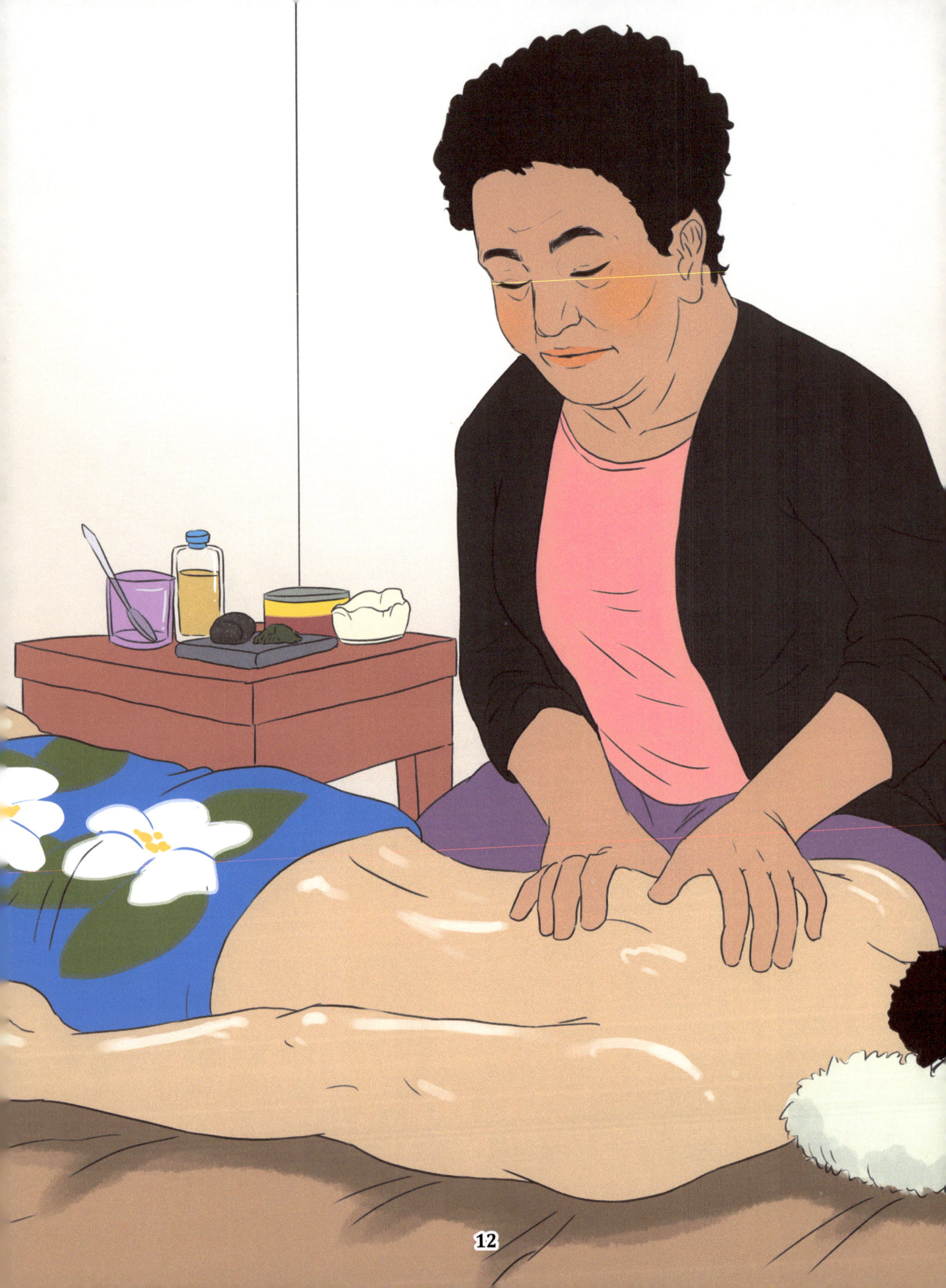

I'm from *fofō*,

baptised by an unspoken type of magic,

with the aroma of Mama's *fagu'u*

casting away any aches and pain.

I'm from *tautua*,

doing *feaus* around the house,

serving trays of *ipu ki* and cabin bread *masi*

to show *fa'aaloalo* to our guests and elders.

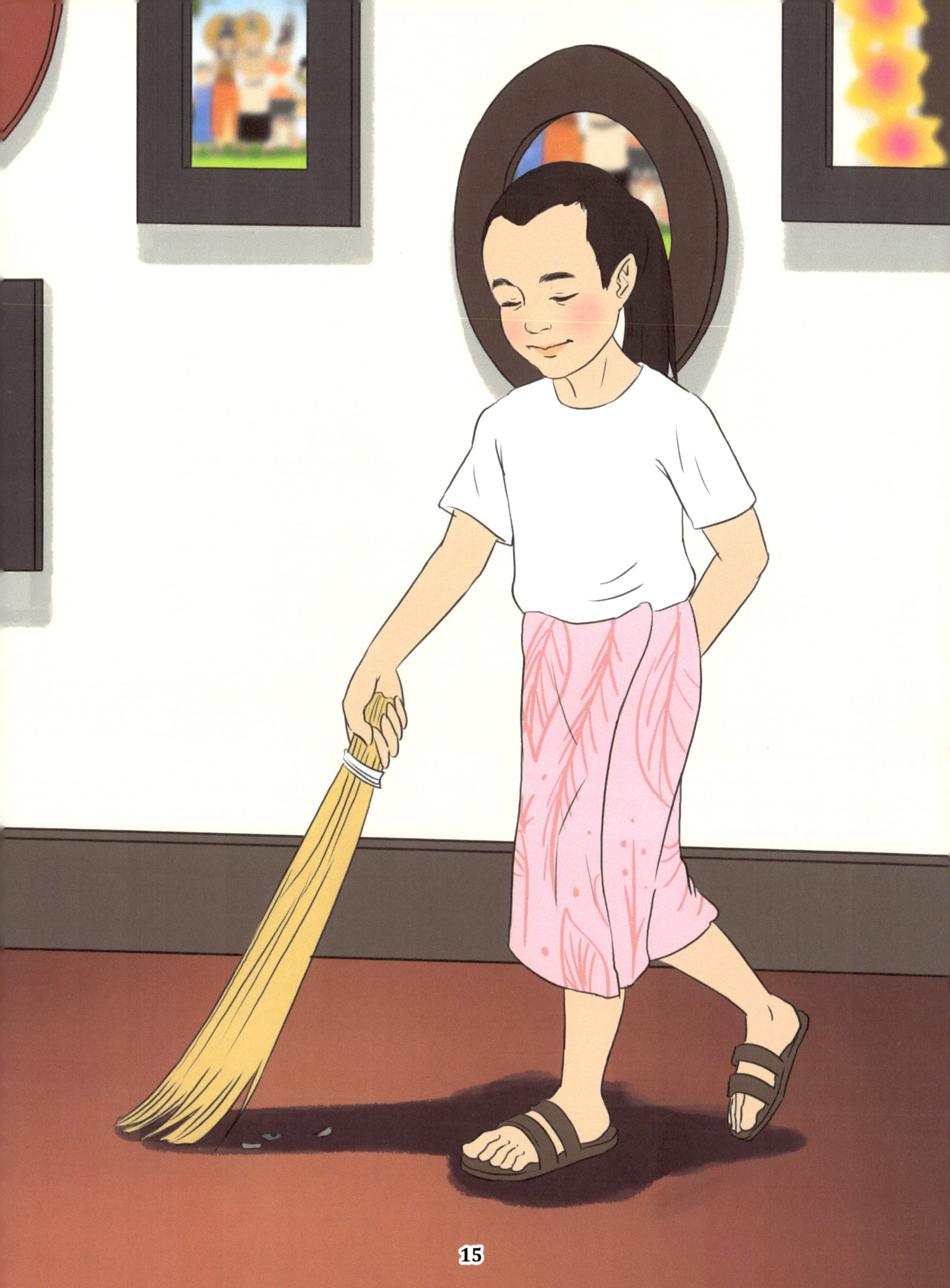

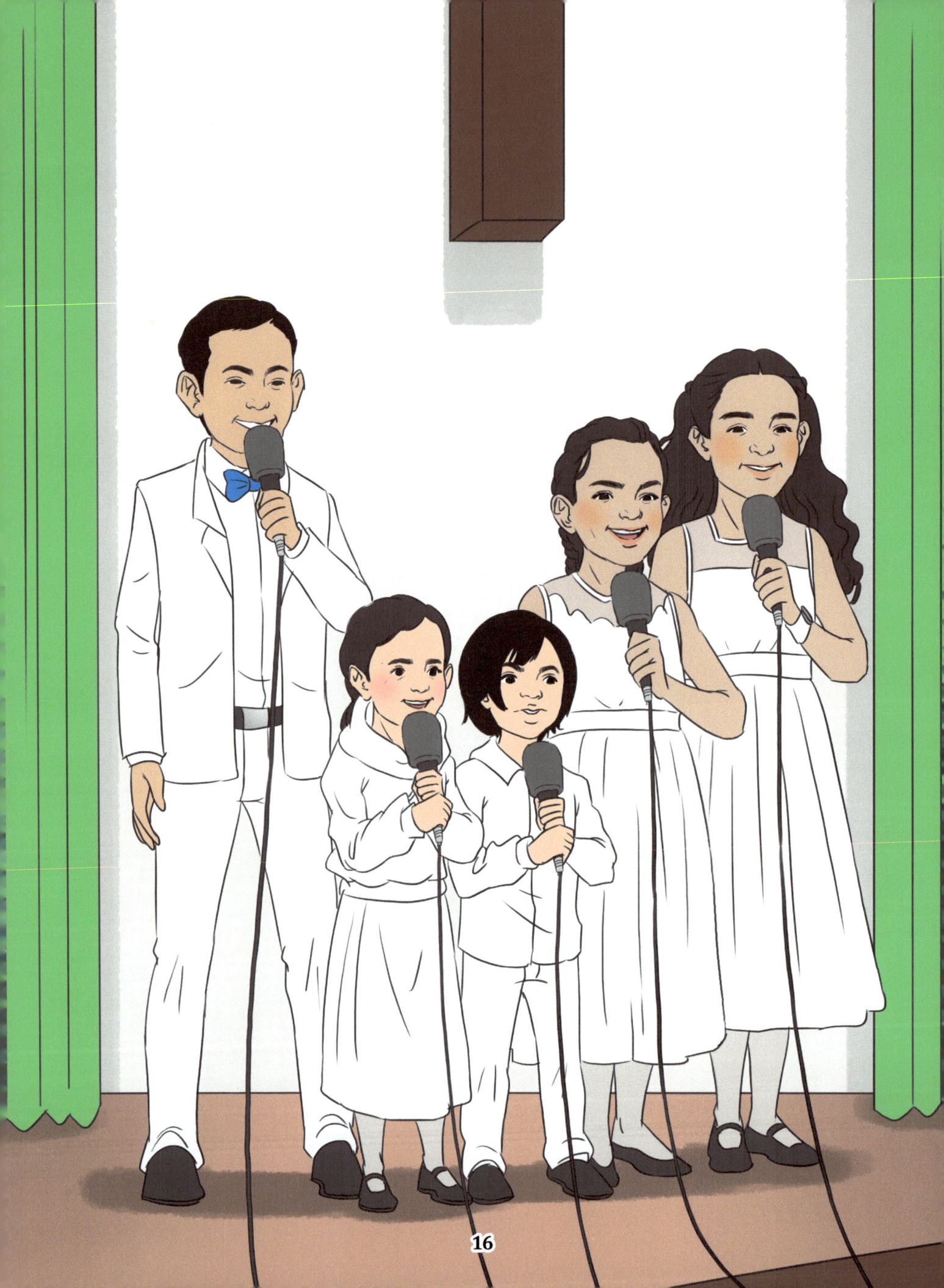

I'm from *lotu tamaiti*,
reciting my *tauloto*
and doing choreography
at Tony-worthy standards.

I'm from the village that raises me,

covered in arms wrapped with *alofa*,

blessed with cousins who are like my siblings,

and aunties and uncles who are our parents too.

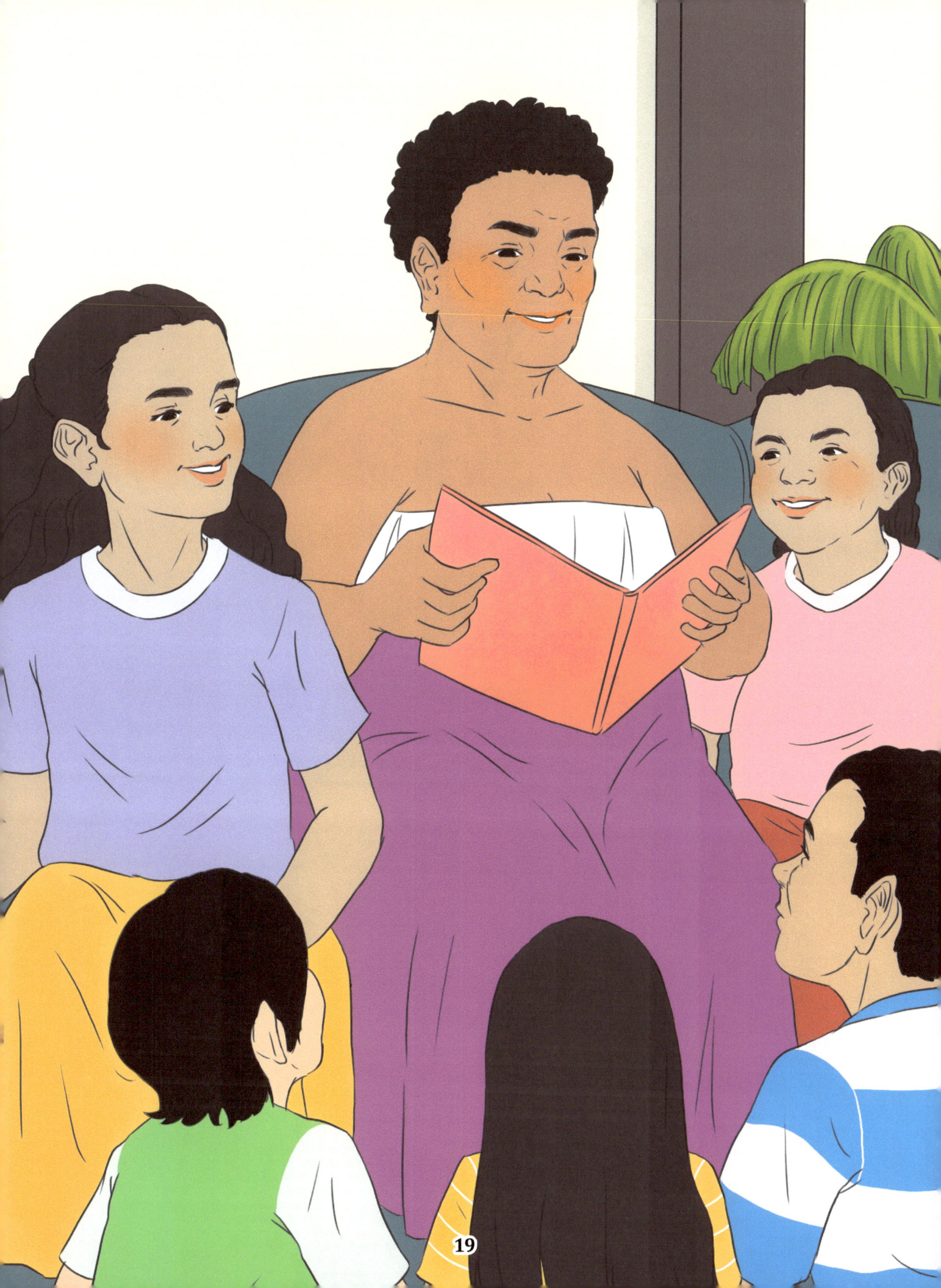

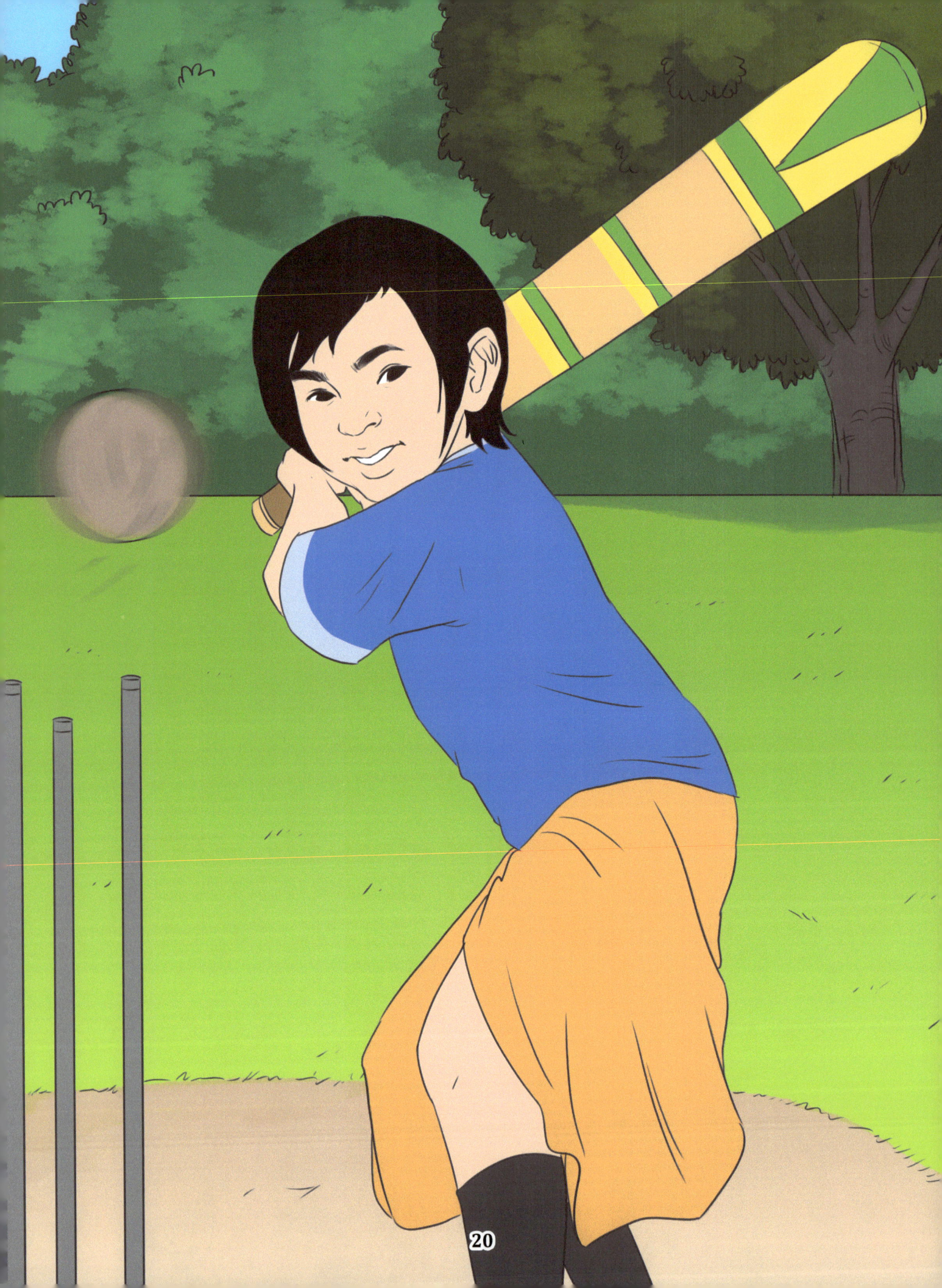

I'm from *kilikiti*,

where chants led by the *faia'oga*

soar from the sidelines

as our *ie lavalava* glides with the wind.

I'm from hunters and fishermen,

living off crops from the *ma'umaga*

and *'i'a* in the sea

that feeds me and my *aiga* plentifully.

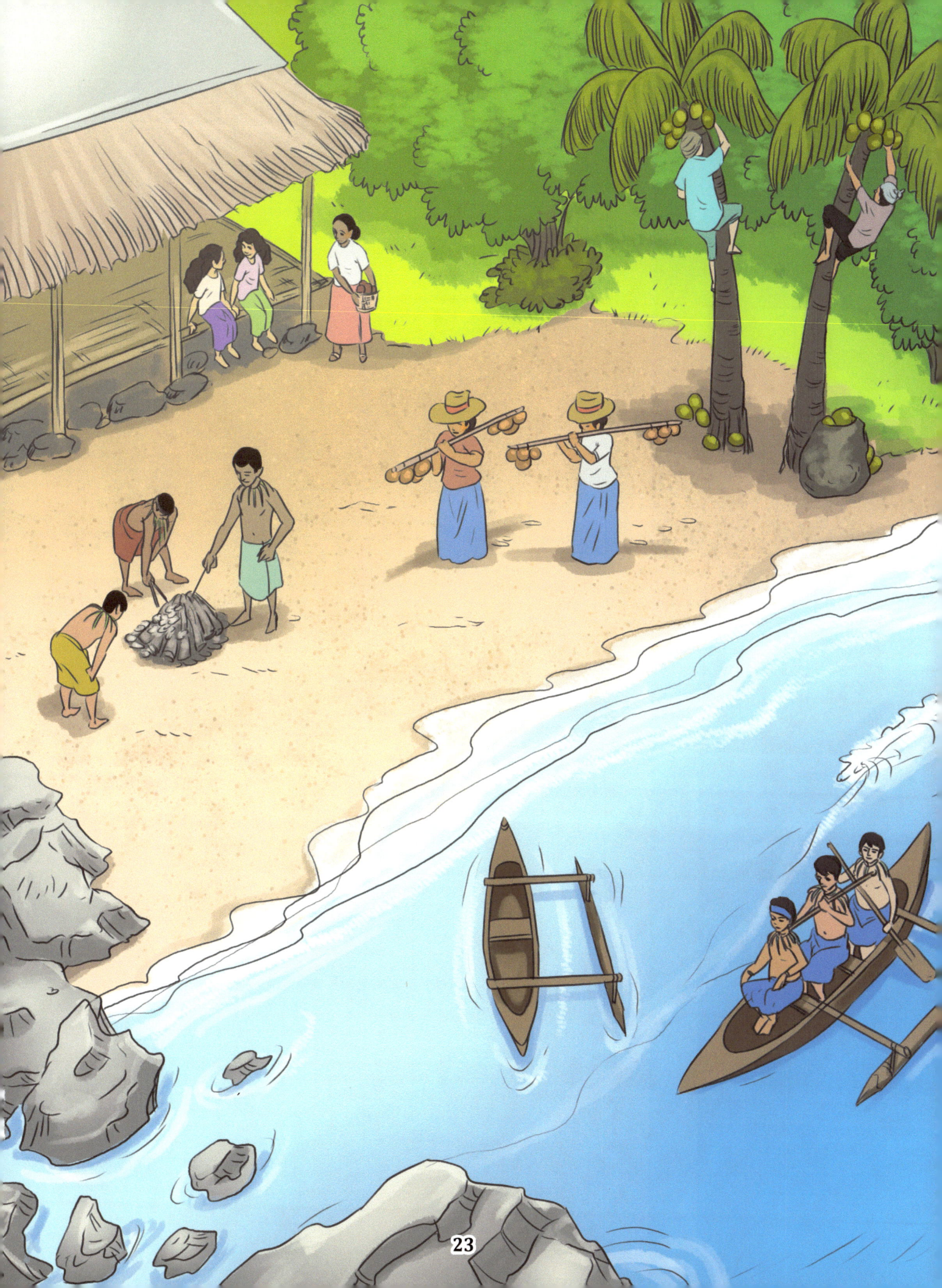

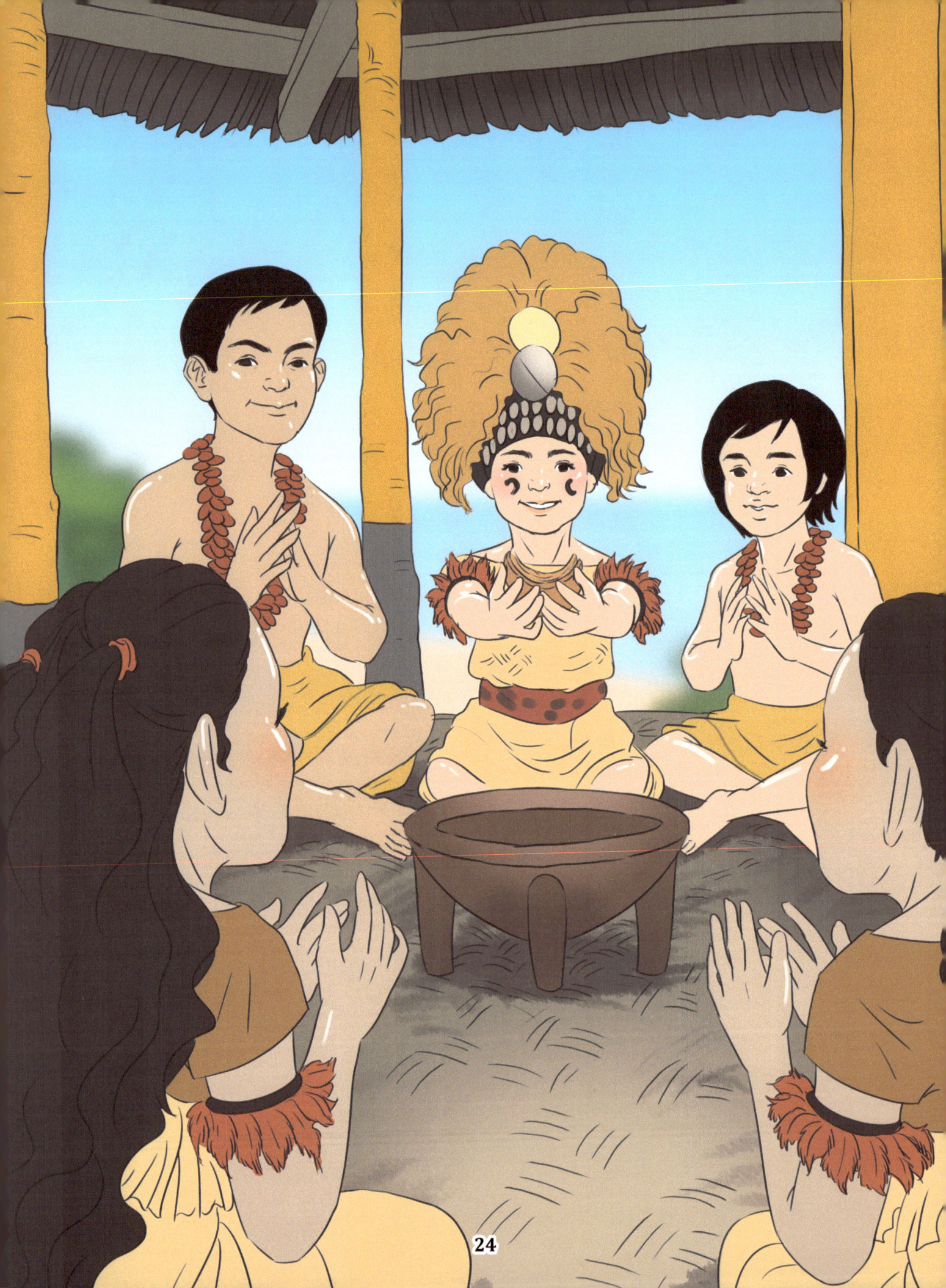

I'm from *tusitala*,

a spoken language of high chiefs and royalty,

to *talanoa* in the mother tongue

and speak myths and legends into existence.

I'm from those who have passed on,

who speak wisdom from the other side.

Sometimes, I see them in my dreams,

as I am their legacy as much as they are mine.

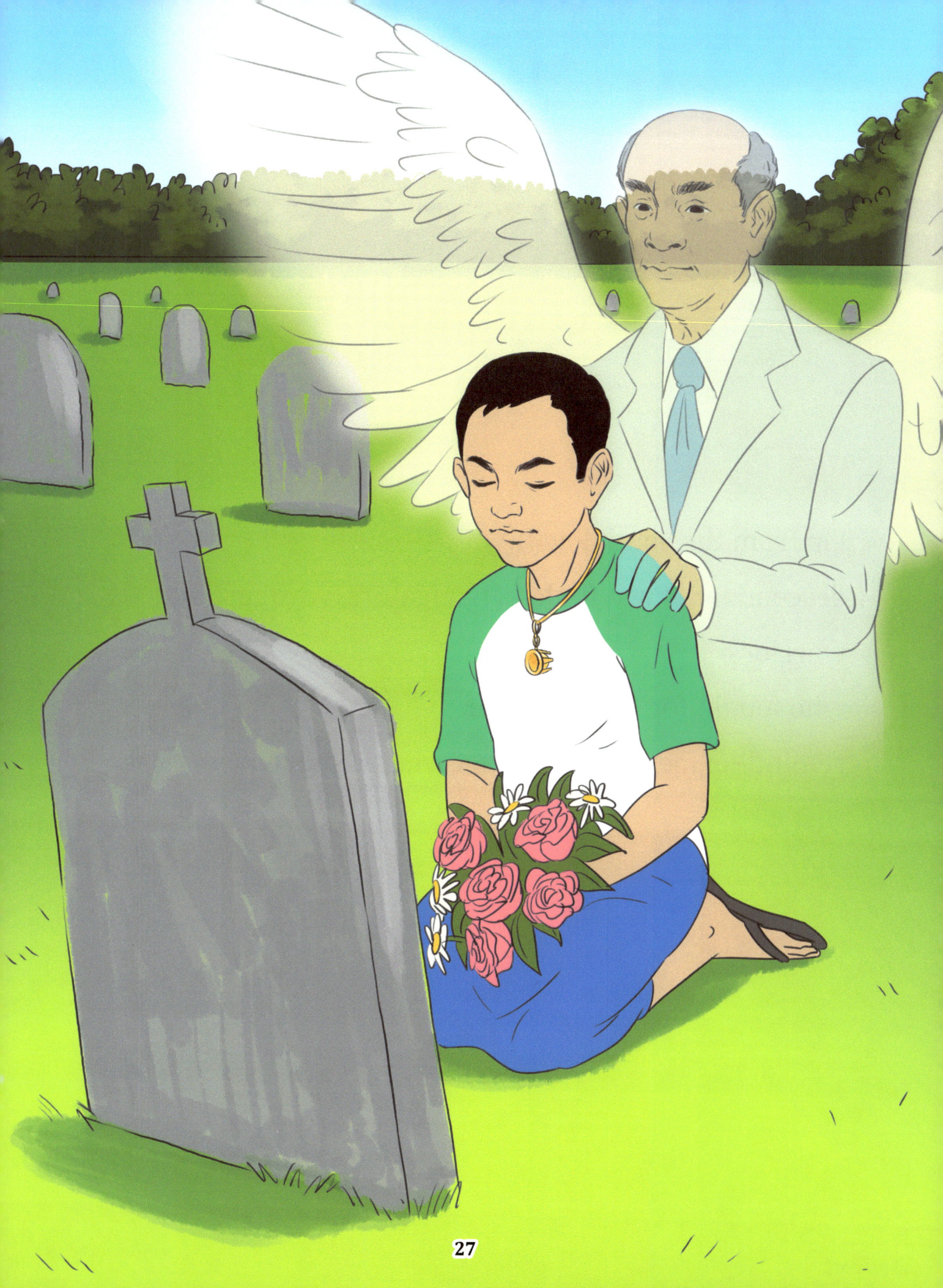

I'm from the South Pacific,

descendant of wayfinders, navigators, voyagers and warriors,

who fought for my existence,

reminding me to never forget where I'm from.

This book is dedicated to Pasifika children across the globe, especially those who live in diasporic countries.

Never forget the Pacific Ocean that runs through your veins.

www.ingramcontent.com/pod-product-compliance
Lightning Source LLC
Chambersburg PA
CBHW051828210526

45473CB00005B/1789